Introduction to Wine and Wine Tasting

I0424825

Green Talent Ltd
Visit my website at www.greentalent.co.uk

Printed in the United States of America

First Printing: 2013

ISBN 978-1-291-29190-2

Index

Table of Contents

Introduction

Wine is fantastic, and so is learning about it, once you start getting the pull from discovering new wines, new aromas, new experiences, the ball starts rolling and does not stop, as with thousands of options available, and many more thousand wines made every year, the road to discovery is endless.

I have been organising, delivering ad enjoying wine tastings for over 15 years now, and I also love educating friends and strangers alike on the wonders of the wine world. I have tasted around 30.000 different wines so far (more or less), and I keep enjoying wine more and more every single day, I would love to share that joy with you.

Year 2009 saw the publishing of my first wine related book, **Wines from Spain**, which was rather technical, with information about grape varieties and wine producing areas, aimed to those who want to become experts or now more about wine producing in Spain, the biggest producer of wine in the world.

With **Introduction to Wine** I am giving you, a simple and easy to understand first step into the wine and wine tasting world. Starting with some basic information about wine production, how to taste it, what to look for in the bottle and in the wine itself,… and the very basics to start enjoying wine and wine tasting.

I have two very clear things about learning (and I am currently working as a lecturer in university): learning step by step and, enjoy and have fun while you learn, and I have tried to reflect this in my book. Hence this is an introductory book, enough information for you to understand wine, and start enjoying drinking it and talking about it.

This book will help you to recognise what is important about wine and wine labels, and will help you to make the most of every wine you try. I am trying to keep this book to around 100 pages, so it is not only easy to read, but it does not take you too long before you can star using the knowledge. It contains enough information, while eliminating all of most of the technicisms; however if you want to now more and increase your knowledge, please check my other books at the end of this one, which contain more specialised and technical information.

I hope you enjoy this book!

Alfredo de la Casa

The Terroir (Soil)

Any present and future wine starts with the terroir, or the soil where the vine is planted and it is astonishing important to determine the wine.

The same grape grown in the same area, sometimes just some meters away, can make two totally different wines due to the different soil. And also different grapes grown in countries far apart can produce two wines that are very similar.

There are certain factors that affect the taste and quality of wine. These include vintage (year of production), climate, location and soil. Also important are the cultivation techniques (viticulture), the producer, and especially the grape variety used.

A **Vintage** is made by weather and not by climate, as the same area tends to have, more or less, the same weather characteristics each year.

Weather and climate directly influence the growth and quality of the grapes. Climate is determined by the location (hence certain area are perfect for wine making) while weather is a result of the nature.

Most wine growing areas are within 30 and 50 latitude and require a combination of frost, heat, sunshine and rain in order to produce the right harvest.

In general, vines will not provide grapes good enough for wine making if the annual mean temperature of the region is below 10 C, being 14 to 15 C the ideal mean temperature.

For vine growing sunshine is needed not only because of the light, but especially because of the heat; approximately 1.300 sunshine hours per season are required, although 1.500 hours are preferred.

A vine usually requires around 68cm of rain per year, with most of the rain falling on spring and winter.

The **location** of the vineyard is essential in determining whether its climate is suitable for viticulture.

Virtually all the world's wine producing areas are located in areas where the mean temperature is between 10 C and 20 C.

Having top quality **soil** is crucial to the vine because it supports the root and the feeding system.

The soil's mineral composition and concentration will influence the growth and acidity of the grapes, and therefore how the wine tastes.

The details of geology and the particulars of how soil affect the growth of vines, although important is not appropriate for this, an initiation to wine book, hence I will not extend on the details.

How is wine made?

Even most of those who know how to taste and enjoy wine, do actually lack key knowledge of how wine is made.

I could write a full book on this subject alone, especially considering the different methods which are available, however, in this introductory book to wine, I will just do that, an introduction, enough to give you basic knowledge of what is important and how the grapes end up in such a fantastic nectar for us enjoy.

First the grapes have to ripe. No ripe enough or too ripe and the wine will suffer the consequences.

For better results, grapes must be picked by hand at the right time and good weather is a must, as poor weather at harvest time can totally ruin the grapes.

After being picked and placed in small containers, grapes are loaded into a small lorry or tractor for then to be taken to the winery where usually there is a hand inspection in order to pick and disregard faulty grapes and debris.

Once selected, grapes go into a machine that cleans the steams, and sometimes crushes them either partially or fully. Grapes travel to the tank to then be pumped into the fermentation vessel.

Red wines are fermented with skins (which give the colour), while white wines are made by pressing the grapes and separating the skin from the juice, which is then fermented.

Grapes are then pressed (traditionally made by foot, but mostly by machine nowadays) so that the juice can then extract colour and other elements from the skins.

The next step is fermentation which can be natural or induced using yeast. Depending on the winery, skins will be pushed to the bottom (mostly to stop bacteria), or wine will be pumped from the bottom on top of the skins.

Once fermentation has taken place, most red wines are put in barrels to complete the maturation process.

The type of oak and whether the barrel has been used before or not, and for how long, will influence the final taste of the wine. While most white wines are stored in steel tanks, red wine can benefit from maturation in oak barrels.

Barrels are then taken to the cellar for a period of 6 months to several years.

On a regular basis the oenologist will check the wines, and in some cases top up the barrels as wine evaporates with time.

Finally the wine is prepared for bottling, sometimes after filtering process.

In some cases the bottles of wine will be put on sale, for most top quality wines they will be kept in the cellar for further in bottle maturation, which could take a few months to many years.

Grape Varieties

The grape or grape variety used to make the wine is likely to be the most influential factor in determining its taste.

However, what does affect the flavour of different grape types?

Skin colour and thickness of the grapes. Dark coloured thick skinned grapes produce very deep coloured wines, while light colour thin skin grapes trend to produce lighter wines.

Size. The smaller the grape, the more concentrated the flavour is.

Structure of the skin. The skin contains itself most of the aromas, hence is very important in the production of wine.

Sugar – Acid ratio. The wine's alcohol will be dictated mostly by the sugar content of the grape, hence its importance.

There are thousands of grape varieties all over the world, sometimes same grapes with different names depending on the countries. In this book I want to cover briefly some of the main grapes.

White Grapes

Chardonnay

One of the most famous white grapes all over the world, used to produce cheap plonks and some of the best wines alike.

Main grape for some of the white Burgundy wines, and also Champagne.

Chenin Blanc

Thin skin and good acidity level, making lovely sweet wines.

Gewrurzraminer

Ge…what? Don't worry, unless you are a German speaker you are likely to mispronounce this grape name.

This grape is very typical from Alsace, but recently re-launched in Australia and even Spain.

It produces very aromatic wines, which tend to be low in acidity.

Muscat

Also known as Muscadet or Moscatel, this grape has a high sugar content, making amazing sweet wines.

Pinot Gris

Another typical Alsace grape, although widely found in Italy (Pinot Griggio).

It is used for producing very complex wines, but rather less intense in Italian sores.

Riesling

Originating from Germany, this grape has recently been added to the New World wine portfolio, with many interesting wines coming from Australia, New Zealand and Chile.

Usually acidic and very mineral, it can nevertheless make fantastic wines.

Sauvignon Blanc

You will other hate or love wines which use this grape.

While some people can smell and taste petrol, most of the rest, including myself, feel that it produces very aromatic perfumed wine which can be a real delight especially those from Marlborough in New Zealand.

Semillon

This grape produces rather dry wines, very common in Sauternes.

Viognier

Traditionally from the Rhone valley in France, is another grape developing in the New World.

Black Grapes

Cabernet Franc

This is one of the Bordeaux typical grapes, and part in some of the most famous and best wines.

Also present in some New World wines, but due to the terroir, still far from producing the amazing wines produced in France. St Emilion and Pomerol are two areas famous for Cabernet Franc based wines

Cabernet Sauvignon

One of the most popular grapes. Cabernet Sauvignon
is another Bordeaux variety, rich in colour, aroma and
depth.

Grenache

Also known as garnacha. Very well known for being the base for Chateauneuf du Pape wines.

Merlot

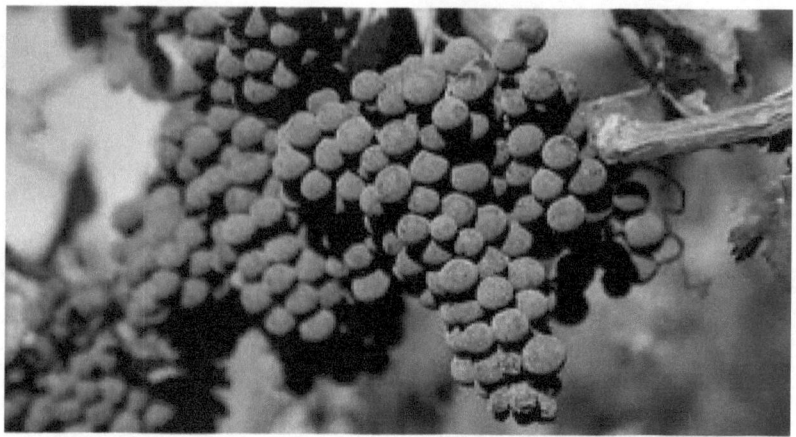

Another of the Bordeaux grapes, merlot makes rich and fruity wines.

Pinot Noir

Very famous in Burgundy and also used in Chile and New Zealand, is another of the either loved or hated grapes.

Pinot Noir can make very aromatic and complex wines, with delicate palate, some of them can be rather sweet or very mineral like those produced in Germany or Oregon.

Tempranillo

This is the most important variety in Rioja, and can produce long lived wines that can age for many years.

Syrah

Also known as Shiraz making rather dark and elegant wines.

How to store wine

Most wines when offered to the public are ready to be drunk, however some others, in particular some French wines, they will benefit from being stored for a few years, as the way they are made it is expected for them to mature further in the bottle.

So how important is how you store wine? It is actually crucial, especially if you are planning to store it for a few years and do not want to have a nasty surprise when you open the bottle.

Regarding storage, there are three things that can turn some of the most expensive wines into vinegar or unpleasant experiences.

First is light. Wine should be kept in dark places with no or next to no light. Direct light can react with some of the wine components and create serious faults in the wine.

Heat is another of the enemies, and wines should be kept in a cool place, usually 11 to 15 degrees for red wines and 9 to 14 degrees for white wines. Ideally wine should be stored on a wine cellar; please note that storing wine in the fridge is not recommended as fridges keep a much lower temperature, which can also damage the wine.

The third enemy is humidity. Either too much, or too little (driving the cork to dry and react with the wine) can damage the wine. Ideally wine should be stored in an environment with 75% humidity.

Something else that also affects the quality of the wine while storing it, and in a negative way, are drastic temperature changes.

Remember, the wine is "alive" and will react to anything, and with most things in nature, any drastic changes are not received well!

Choosing the wine glasses

A glass is a glass isn't it? It is but the taste and overall feeling of drinking wine, could change depending which glass you use.

There are many different types of wine glasses, varying in size, shape and quality, which will affect your experience of enjoying wine.

Glassware can affect wine appreciation, it influences how you perceive the colour, aromas and taste.

When choosing the wine glasses for your wine, first you need to make sure that they are **clean and clear** and no tinted glass, as otherwise will affect the visual of the wine.

As you will learn a bit later the colour and the information the colour and intensity that can give you about the wine, is part of the enjoyment of tasting wine. The clearer the glass, the easier to appreciate the wine's colour, intensity and uniformity.

A thin rim will make your senses concentrate more on the wine than on the glass.

Another important consideration is glass **size**. The bowl should be big enough for an appropriate amount to be poured, and to allow for the wine to be swirled in order to oxygenate it.

A large bowl and a narrow opening help to magnify the aromas, allowing aromas to expand on the bowl, but not much room for them to escape through the opening.

It is also recommended that the glass has a steam, for the drinker to hold it, so that any dirt on the fingers does not stain the glass, but also in order not to pass excess body heat to the wine.

Different styles of wines require different types of glasses in order to enjoy them at their most.

In general, sparkling wines are best if served in flute shaped glasses. Red wines require larger bowls as they evolve better with larger amounts of oxygen, while white wines are better served in smaller size glasses.

Matching the glass to the wine

Riedel, who we have to thanks for most of the following pictures, and who is probably the best manufacturer of top quality wine (and spirits) glasses, has spent several decades studying what size and shape gets the best out of each grape type and area.

They have different collections, some of them with 40 different shapes.

I once attended a course with them in London, and it is incredible how the same wine will taste different depending the glass you use to drink it from.

These are some examples, of what goes better with, and if you can afford it, you should aim to get a set of good quality wine glasses to match your drinking habits.

Albarino

Amarone

Barolo

Bordeaux

Cabernet Franc

Cabernet Sauvignon

Chablis

Champagne

Chardonnay

Chenin Blanc

Chianti

Cognac

Merlot

Pinot Blanc/grigio/ gris

Pinot noir

Port

Riesling

Sangiovese

Sauvignon Blanc

Semillion

Sherry

Shiraz, Syrah

Tempranillo

Viognier

Zinfandel

How to open and serve wine

Serving wine may be thought of something straight forward like open and pour, however, it isn't always the case.

Generally speaking, wine bottles have one of these three different bottle closures: screw cap, cork, plastic cork.

There have been extensive discussions about what type of bottle closure is better, and so far no agreement has been reached.

Some prefer **screw cap** (which is considerably cheaper than the other options, and hence saving money to the manufacturer, but not necessarily to the customer), claiming that by using them the wine will never be affected but defects in the cork; however they tend to forget mentioning that defects on the screw cap can seriously ruin the wine too.

Another problem is that screw caps do not allow air to enter the bottle, so those wines which need it to evolve and become better will not benefit if using this system.

Natural cork defenders, claim that the traditional method is the best, as it allows enough but not too much air to enter the bottle which is ideal in order for some wines to evolve while maturing in bottles, which is true, however if the cork has defects or if it dries out it could also ruin the wine.

Finally **artificial cork** defenders, made in a similar size and shape to traditional corks but at a fraction of the cost, claim that they have advantages of both previous systems, with none of the disadvantages, which is not really true, as the amount of air they let in is not the same as traditional corks, and at the end of the day, your wine will be in touch with a plastic derivative.

I have opened thousands of bottles, with very few of them corked, so I personally refer traditional corks and I do prefer to pay the extra money, as I believe that the wine is kept in better conditions, when bottled using natural corks.

Most bottles will be covered with a plastic or similar capsule, which is recommended to be removed (preferably by cutting it around the neck of the bottle) before the bottle is opened.

Screw caps just need to be unscrewed, while you should use a cork screw to open the bottles with a cork (artificial or not).

For bottles closed with a cork, it is important that you check the size of the cork before using the cork screw, making sure than when screwing it in the bottle, it does not reach the end, as otherwise small pieces of cork will end up in your bottle, and then in your glass, which is rather unpleasant!

Once opened, pour a small taste and check it to make sure the wine is in good condition before serving and enjoying it!

Wine serving temperature

Serving temperature and glassware can seriously affect the wine's aromas and flavours, as well as your overall opinion of it, if you don't believe me, try and serve the same wine at different temperatures and see: a red wine served too cold will lose a lot of its aromas, while a white wine too warm may be too overwhelming as heat could destroy the balance between different aromas.

Light dry and crisp white wines should be served 7 to 10 degrees Celsius in order to keep its freshness and fruit aromas.

Light fruity reds and full bodied/oaky whites should be served 10 to 15 degrees, while

Full boy reds are ideal when served at around 15 to 18 degrees.

Remember temperature before serving, and have in mind that for sparkling or white wine which is kept at room temperature, it may take up to two hours in the fridge to reach the ideal temperature (and freezer is not an option!); while for a red that has been kept in the fridge, it may need up to 45 minutes to warm up by itself before is ready to be served.

Decanting wine

With age many wines develop a natural deposit of tannins and pigments that are collected in the bottom of the bottle, in the case of white wines, sometimes even crystal deposit is formed. These deposits are harmless, however can spoil the experience. One of the ways of getting rid of them is to decant the wine before serving.

Another reason for decanting the wine (pouring it from the bottle into a decanter) is to allow the wine to "breath".

Allowing the wine to breath will create a rapid maturation, developing some of its aromas and flavours by allowing it to oxygenate.

Before decanting the wine, the bottle should be placed into an upright position for several hours, in order for the sediment lying on the side to go to the bottom.

Tasting the wine

If you want to make the most of the experience of discovering a wine, the first rule of tasting is NOT to check the bottle and the label, as it can really influence your opinion of the wine even before tasting it.

Once opened, you may wish to check the cork for clues of whether it has affected the wine. Having said that I have seen corks that look clean and perfect, but the wine was corked and likewise, I have seen corks totally stained that looked had ruined the wine to find it being perfect.

Once poured on a clean glass, you should inspect the wine, the colour and intensity can give you an idea of the age and whether or not has been kept in oak barrels for white wines.

For white wines, although the type of grape can influence this, the darker the colour the longer the age of the wine, so if you are seeing a very pale wine, it is likely that is a rather young wine.

Wines being matured in oak barrels can also add darkness and intensity to the colour.

Likewise for red wines, oak barrel and age, as well as grapes used can make darker looking wines. Although in general age will make red wines look more brownish.

Look at the wine, especially at the edges and see if colour changes from centre to edges, here is no real link between colour, intensity and quality, but most people love uniformity in their wines.

Next step is to smell the wine. I prefer to have an initial nose before swirling the wine, just for my own curiosity to see how the wine changes after swirling.

The main reason for swirling is for the wine to have higher contact with air, and hence oxygen and with more space allow the aromas to open up and reach your nose easily.

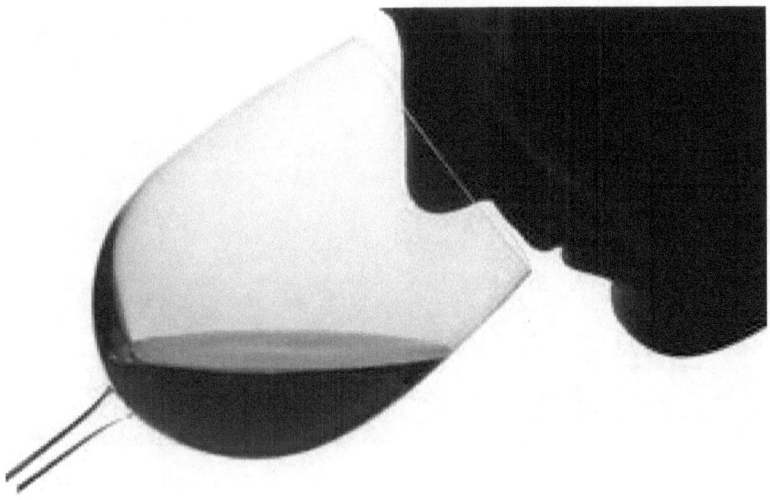

Get your nose as close to the wine as possible in order to try to isolate its aromas from anything else present in the room, and try to analyse what you feel, what you get.

For inexperienced wine tasters, it may take a few months and good practice to start getting the different flavours and aromas that different wines can provide.

After swirling or drinking you may find some "tears" or "legs" coming down the glass. There are different theories for this: some experts consider tears to be the result of high alcohol content, although I know several low alcohol wines leaving tears. While other experts associate the tears with more full body wines, which tend to be accurate in many cases, but not always.

However the most probable reason for legs is a high content of glycerol in the wine.

The next step is to take a sip of the wine. But don't drink it as yet! Let it flow around your mouth so that all taste buds get the chance to feel the wine.

What do you get? Also pay attention to the texture, the silkness or lack of it, the body and the intensity.

In theory, you do not need to drink the wine to have a full appreciation, or so many experts say. I however disagree because although you will experience and feel most if not all flavours without having to swallow, is with swallowing when you will be able to assess the acidity and sometimes measure the length.

The length is how long you get the flavours/taste of the wine in your mouth after you have either drunk it or spit it. The longer the length the better, because you are paying good money for your wines, and you want the experience of each sip to last as long as possible.

Wines can have many different scents, see next chapters for examples, depending on the grapes used, vinification, etc.

Wines however have four basic components: taste, alcohol, tannins and acidity.

A good wine will have a good balance of the above four characteristics; too much alcohol or acidity or even tannin can make the wine rather unpleasant, and bad or indifferent taste will make the wine blunt and uninteresting.

In plain words, tannin is what causes the dry, astringent feeling in the mouth after drinking certain wines.

There are two main sources of tannins in wine. First oak if the wine is matured in wine barrels, with time it may get some tannin from it. However the main origin for tannin in wine is that they are present in the skin, stem and seeds of the grapes, which explains what is more likely to find tannin in red wine (which are made by crushing the full grapes and sometimes stems) than in white wines, which are made by fermenting just the juice.

Tannins are important as they provide colour, structure and flavour. In general wines with a lot of tannins are meant to be aged; with time the tannins will reduce while providing the wine with more body and structure.

There are four main types of acid present in wine, and their mission is to help preserve the wine, and also help to shape flavours and after taste giving it structure.

Aromas in wine

According to Le Nez du Vin, which sells aroma kits to help understand aromas in wine, you can find some or many of the following aromas in different wines:

1 Lemon
2 Grapefruit
3 Orange
4 Pineapple
5 Banana
6 Lychee
7 Melon
8 Muscat
9 Apple
10 Pear
11 Quince
12 Strawberry
13 Raspberry
14 Redcurrant
15 Blackcurrant
16 Bilberry
17 Blackberry
18 Cherry
19 Apricot
20 Peach
21 Almond (kernel)
22 Prune
23 Walnut
24 Hawthorn
25 Acacia

26 Linden

27 Honey

28 Rose

29 Violet

30 Green pepper

31 Mushroom

32 Truffle

33 Yeast

34 Cedar

35 Pine

36 Liquorices

37 Blackcurrant bud

38 Cut hay

39 Thyme

40 Vanilla

41 Cinnamon

42 Clove

43 Pepper

44 Saffron

45 Leather

46 Musk

47 Butter

48 Toasted bread

49 Roasted almonds

50 Roasted hazelnut

51 Caramel

52 Coffee

53 Dark chocolate

54 Smoked

Tastes in wine

This is a non-comprehensive list of the most common wine flavours:

Almonds
Apple
Apricot
Asparagus
Banana
Black Currant
Black pepper
Blackberry
Boysenberry
Cherry
Cinnamon
Cloves
Cocoa
Coffee
Currant
Fig
General berry
General citrus
General nuttiness
General wood
Gooseberry
Grass
Hazelnut
Leather
Liquorice
Lychee

Mango
Melon
Mint
Mocha
Oak
Orange
Peach
Pear
Pepper
(white/black)
Plum
Raisin
Raspberry
Rose
Smoke
Strawberry
Tea
Toast
Tobacco
Vanilla
Violet

Common tastes associated to particular wines

This is just a very generic analogy, but shared by many people. The following are some commonly found tastes associated to some particular grapes:

Chardonnay: tropical fruits, pine apple, mangoes, lemons, citrus, melon, apple, pear, peach, apricots.

Sauvignon Blanc: grapefruit, lime, lemons

Cabernet Franc and Cabernet Sauvignon: cherries, black currant, black fruits, spices

Merlot: plums, red fruits, raspberries, black currants

Syrah, Shiraz: black fruits, black pepper.

Pinot Noir: red fruits, flowers, herbs.

Zinfandel: black fruits and spices.

Reading the label

Labels can be both misleading and helpful in order to choose wine. When buying wine I always take label information with a pinch of salt: some producers, aiming to increase their sales sometimes by confusing shoppers, add some information to labels which is just misleading, incorrect or simply means nothing apart from in the minds of some buyers who know little about wine.

Some examples are:

- Some people associate the word "chateau" in wine labels (especially in French wines) with good quality wine. First, it is just a word, and you can call any wine chateau.... And it means nothing. The true meaning of chateau is castle.

- Reserve, Reserva, Riserva and similar are also associated with good quality wines. However with the exception of French, Italian and some Spanish wines (where such words guarantee some maturation times among other things) those words, especially in new world wine labels, mean absolutely nothing.

So what to look for in a wine label? Well, there are five main things to look for:

1) **Vintage** or the year when the wine was produced. This may give you a clue of when is best to drink the wine, especially on certain high quality French wines which reach their best after 10 or 15 years.

2) **Grape variety,** it will help you to assess the complexity and body of the wine.

3) **Region**, will give you hints of the intensity, flavour and style, for example Burgundy wines.

4) **Alcohol level**: will help you determine the body and sweetness level of the wine. Sweeter and lighter wines do usually have low alcohol levels, while dry and full bodied wines have higher levels of alcohol.

5) **Producer**: can tell you about the consistency and quality of the wine.

Sample wine labels

Chablis Grand Cru

LES CLOS

APPELLATION CHABLIS GRAND CRU CONTRÔLÉE

Récolte 2004

Domaine Pascal Bouchard

Pascal Bouchard à Chablis, France

PRODUIT DE FRANCE

750 ml.

Alc. 13 % vol.

FENESTRA

2001
TORRONTES

LODI
SILVASPOONS VINEYARDS

ALC. 12.0% BY VOL.

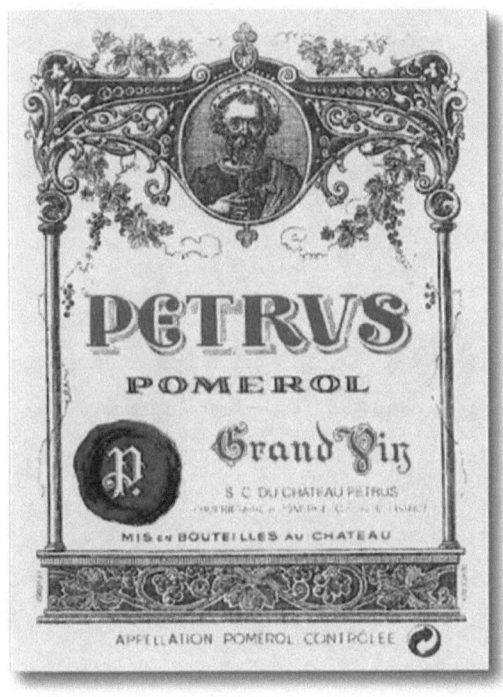

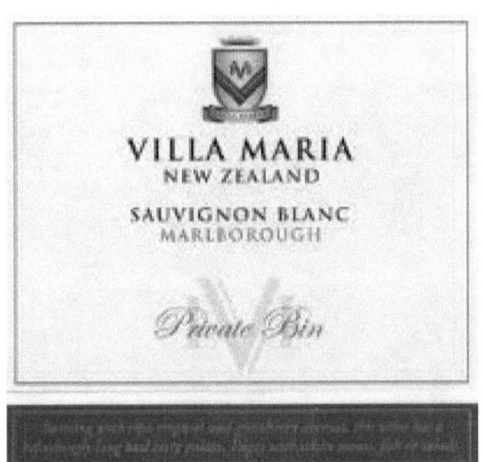

Wine tasting common terms

Aroma: the wine's smell

Balance: the combination of acidity, tannins, alcohol and sweetness in the wine.

Body: the feeling of weight and size in the wine. Full bodied wines for examples feel heavier and stronger.

Complexity: the depth of wine made out of aromas, flavours, intensity, harmony and overall feeling.

Decant: to transfer the wine from the bottle to another recipient (usually a different bottle named decanter), with the aim of bringing the wine in contact with oxygen and getting rid of residues.

Depth: complexity and concentration of flavours

Finish: final impression or aftertaste of the wine, after being swallowed or spat.

Nose: the wine's smell, also known as aroma.

Palate: the flavour or taste of the wine

Sulfites: some elements produced as part of fermentation present in virtually every wine.

Tannin: substance or element found in in grape seeds and stems giving a feeling of dryness in the mouth.

Vintage: the year the grapes were harvested to make the wine.

What next?

This is the first of a series of books aimed to educate those of you interested in wine, helping you to learn about wine and wine tasting and enjoy them more.

Please visit www.greentalent.co.uk and expect the following titles soon:

French wines.

Spanish wines.

Italian wines.

New World wines.

Some other books from Green Talent

All books are available from the following international retailers:

Vietnam Business and People: understanding cultural differences

Alfredo de la Casa

With this book, and using my experience in settling in Viet Nam, I try to help future expats or even tourists to make the most out of Viet Nam, with minimum difficulties to achieve their objectives, this being to communicate with a pharmacist or the lucky money protocol in Tet.

I am also including a lot of information on cultural differences, as problems can easily be reached without knowing due to some drastic cultural differences between Vietnamese ways and Western ways. I have divided the book in small chapters so that it is easy to find various subjects.

The book can be read in any order as each chapter is independent. I hope you find it helpful and enjoy reading it!

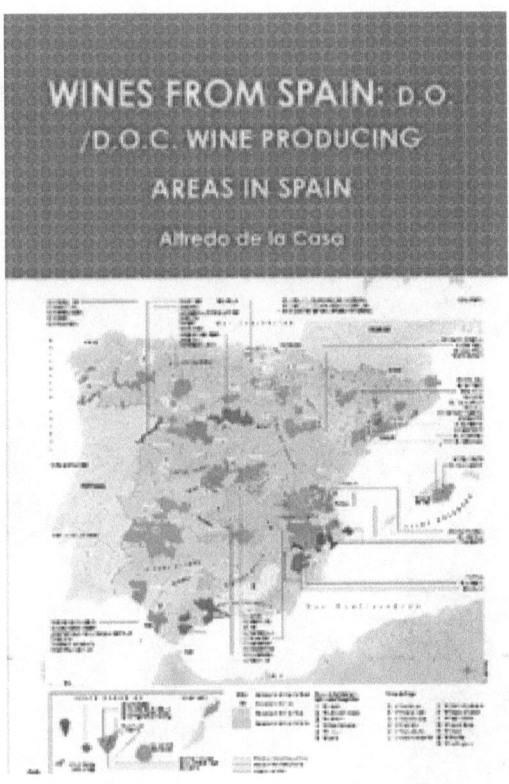

A concise easy to read book with information of all the wine producing areas in Spain, including description of the various origin denominations, grapes, production surface and much more.

I could write a lot about what I think you should see and visit around Malaysia, however, an image is better than a thousand words, and here I am presenting you with over 340 pictures of beautiful Malaysia, which I am sure are better than 340.000 words, for you to see, judge and hopefully encourage you to visit Malaysia

Restaurants: How to eat well in London at low prices.

Alfredo de la Casa

In this book I am presenting my favourite 99 restaurants around London. I love eating, I love eating good food even more, and if I have to pay little for it and a good service is provided, that is what I call perfection. It is not very difficult to find a good restaurant serving good food if you are willing to pay £70 or more per person. This book is not about that type of eateries, but the opposite: after having lived for 13 years in London I have tried many restaurants, some good some not so good, here I have collated those I think you should try, with a special mention to my top 10 favourites.

The guide for the wise traveller who wants the best!
18,748 Words, 235 Pages, 184 Pictures, 140
Reviews. Although I initially arrived as a tourist to
Vietnam, I was enchanted by its magic, and decided
to quit my job in London and move here, and since I
have done nothing but enjoy the gratitude and
kindness of its people. When I visited as a tourist I
brought three tourist guides, none of which really

satisfied me, so I decided to write this one. If you are a similar traveller to me, I am sure you will enjoy the lack of clutter to fill pages, writing about what is important, and lots of tips that usually only locals know about. This book will bring you to most interesting parts of Ho Chi Minh City, as well as to other parts of the country. Do not worry if you think I am not covering everything and you will be short of things to do and see: if you visit everything I review in this book, you will need three to four weeks! I HOPE YOU ENJOY IT!

About the author

Alfredo de la Casa i of best selling books, includ d people: understandi

De la Casa was bor ere he graduated as a Man wever his passions have a lling, cultural differences fine food and wine).

He has travel to over 26 countries including Mexico, Cuba, Portugal, Spain, Tunisia, Malaysia, Thailand, Cambodia, Vietnam, Sweden, France, Germany, Italy, Poland, Hungary and Croatia. While he has worked and lived in three, and he is now a resident in Viet Nam and a regular writer for the local press.

His passions, experience and communication skills have provided him with the right background and tools to be an expert in cultural differences, travel and hospitality which is clearly reflected in the quality of his articles, books and seminars.

www.ingramcontent.com/pod-product-compliance
Lightning Source LLC
Chambersburg PA
CBHW031239280526
45784CB00004B/1641